Puffy Pig, little Fuzzy Bear, Gaga Duck,
Witty Donkey all live together in the "Happy
time, they get along harmoniously and enjoy living together.

Puffy Pig is the youngest, and everyone loves him very much. However, sometimes Puffy Pig can be a little bossy, which makes his friends less willing to play with him.One day, Puffy Pig bought a new toy airplane and went out to the lawn to play. He noticed that Fuzzy Bear was also playing with an airplane, and Fuzzy Bear's plane was the latest remote-controlled model. The best thing about a remote-controlled airplane is that you can make it fly up and down just by holding the controller.

Puffy Pig felt very envious and walked over to Fuzzy Bear, saying, "Fuzzy Bear, let's swap airplanes."Fuzzy Bear didn't want to and said, "Why swap? I haven't played with my new plane enough! I'll let you play with it later!" Puffy Pig was unhappy and bossily replied, "Your plane is better than mine, so we have to swap!" Fuzzy Bear became angry and shouted, "I'm not swapping with you!"

Seeing that Fuzzy Bear refused to swap, Puffy Pig snatched Fuzzy Bear's plane and ran away. Fuzzy Bear chased after him, shouting, "Puffy Pig, give me back my plane! Hurry and return my plane!"

When Puffy Pig saw Fuzzy Bear coming after him, he angrily threw the plane onto the lawn. Although the plane didn't break, Fuzzy Bear was very upset because it was his favorite plane! From then on, Fuzzy Bear didn't want to play with Puffy Pig anymore.

Sometimes, Puffy Pig would play with Gaga Duck, maybe because Gaga Duck is a girl, and Puffy Pig wasn't as bossy. One day, Gaga Duck was jumping rope on the lawn. Puffy Pig ran over and said, "Let's jump rope together."

Gaga Duck agreed. To show off, Puffy Pig jumped very fast and said, "I can jump thirty times. Pretty cool, huh?" Gaga Duck didn't agree and said, "I can jump forty times." Puffy Pig felt challenged and exaggerated, "I can jump fifty times!" Gaga Duck wasn't backing down, "I can jump eighty times." Puffy Pig said, "Let's have a race to see who can jump faster."

Gaga Duck smiled mysteriously and said, "Let's not just jump rope. Look, there's a swing over there. Whoever reaches it last loses." With that, Gaga Duck ran off, and Puffy Pig chased after her as fast as he could.

They played together all morning. They pushed each other on swings, played on the seesaw, hid and sought, jumped, ran, and laughed...

Although they had some minor disagreements, they had a lot of fun. Witty Donkey saw Gaga Duck and Puffy Pig having such a good time and felt relieved because Puffy Pig usually didn't play with his friends for so long.

After lunch, Gaga Duck still wanted to play. She asked Puffy Pig and Fuzzy Bear, "Do you want to play a teacher and student game?" "Yes, yes! Let's start right away," Puffy Pig eagerly replied. Fuzzy Bear thought for a moment and said, "Yes, I do too."

Gaga Duck said, "Then hurry back to your rooms and bring your backpacks and books to the living room so we can play together." Puffy Pig and Fuzzy Bear ran back to their rooms and brought their backpacks and books to the living room. Gaga Duck also brought her backpack, books, stationery, and a few dolls to the living room.

The three set up tables and chairs. Gaga Duck placed the dolls on small stools as students, used a cabinet as a podium, hung a blackboard, and set out some chalk and a pointer. Everything was ready. Puffy Pig was very excited and thought, "This is going to be so much fun! I definitely want to be the teacher!"

Gaga Duck, Fuzzy Bear, sit down! It's time for class. Today I will teach you Chinese pinyin, starting with the first letter, A. Puffy Pig began the lesson seriously. "Wait! Why are you the teacher? I want to be the teacher, and I learn better than you," Gaga Duck protested.

Gaga Duck, sit down quickly, or I'll have to use the pointer to discipline the misbehaving student, Puffy Pig said, picking up the pointer to scold Gaga Duck. Nearby, Fuzzy Bear shouted, "Puffy Pig, what are you doing? If you keep acting like this, we won't want to play with you anymore!"

If you don't want to play, fine! What's the big deal? I don't want to play with you guys anyway! Puffy Pig threw down the pointer, packed up his backpack and books, and stormed back to his room angrily. Gaga Duck cried sadly, "Puffy Pig is too bossy, I won't play games with him anymore." Fuzzy Bear saw Gaga Duck's sadness and said, "Yes, from now on we won't play games with Puffy Pig."

The next day, during breakfast, neither Gaga Duck nor Fuzzy Bear spoke to Puffy Pig. Witty Donkey and Hoppy Bunny thought, "They were having so much fun yesterday, why aren't they talking today?"

After breakfast, Gaga Duck and Fuzzy Bear happily played on the swings together. Puffy Pig sulkily went back to his room alone.

Witty Donkey went to Puffy Pig's room and asked with concern, "Puffy Pig, why aren't you going out to play with them?" Puffy Pig angrily replied, "Gaga Duck and Fuzzy Bear are too bossy and unreasonable. I won't play with them anymore! Witty Donkey brother, will you play with me instead?" Witty Donkey said, "Puffy Pig, I have a lot to do and can't always play with you. Can you tell me how they are being bossy?" But Puffy Pig could only stammer, "I... I..."

Witty Donkey said, "If only one friend doesn't want to play, it might be normal. But if two, three, four, or even more friends don't want to play with you, you should think about whether you did something wrong and why everyone doesn't want to play with you." Puffy Pig's face turned red. He lowered his head and thought for a long time before saying, "I was wrong. I shouldn't have only thought about myself while playing and not considered others." Witty Donkey said, "We are all members of Happy Haven. We are a family and must get along nicely. If you did something wrong, shouldn't you bravely admit it?" Puffy Pig nodded and said, "Yes."

Witty Donkey smiled and said, "Shouldn't Puffy Pig apologize to Gaga Duck and Fuzzy Bear for his mistake?" Puffy Pig thought for a moment and said, "Yes, if I admit my mistake, they will forgive me, and we can play together again, right?" Witty Donkey nodded...

Hoppy Bunny went to Gaga Duck's room and found Fuzzy Bear and Gaga Duck playing with a Rubik's Cube. They were happy to see Hoppy Bunny and said, "Hoppy Bunny sister, let's play with the Rubik's Cube together?" Hoppy Bunny smiled and said, "Why don't you go play with Puffy Pig? He's really good at the Rubik's Cube too." Gaga Duck and Fuzzy Bear looked at each other and told Hoppy Bunny what happened yesterday.

Hoppy Bunny said, "We live together, so we can't completely reject someone just because of a small mistake. Think about it, isn't Puffy Pig much nicer than before? At least he gets up on time and tidies his room regularly, and everyone helped with that. Now that he made a mistake, we should help him fix it too." Fuzzy Bear said, "Yes, but Puffy Pig doesn't think he did anything wrong." Gaga Duck said, "Actually, I was wrong too. I should bravely admit my mistakes."

While they were discussing, the doorbell rang. Gaga Duck opened the door and saw Puffy Pig standing there. He looked down and said to Gaga Duck and Fuzzy Bear, "I'm sorry, Fuzzy Bear. I shouldn't have broken your plane. I'm sorry, Gaga Duck. I shouldn't have only thought about my own fun during the game and ignored everyone else."

Gaga Duck and Fuzzy Bear quickly replied, "It's okay, it's okay. We're still friends." "Puffy Pig, would you like to play the Rubik's Cube with us?" Gaga Duck asked. Puffy Pig said, "Of course I would!" So, the three happily played together. The members of Happy Home got along even better.